HAL•LEONARD®
TRUMPET
PLAY-ALONG

AUDIO
ACCESS
INCLUDED

VOL. 6

MILES DAVIS

Photo by David Redfern/Redferns/Getty

Musicians:
Trumpet – Jamie Breiwick
Saxophone – Jason Weber
Drums – Devin Drobka
Bass – John Christensen
Piano – Mark Davis

Produced by Chris Kringel
Mixed by Kyle White

To access audio visit:
www.halleonard.com/mylibrary

Enter Code
4791-1103-3068-0016

ISBN 978-1-4950-0017-1

Visit Hal Leonard Online at
www.halleonard.com

HAL•LEONARD®
CORPORATION
7777 W. BLUEMOUND RD. P.O. BOX 13819
MILWAUKEE, WISCONSIN 53213

MILES DAVIS

CONTENTS

Airegin

By Sonny Rollins

D

E

Bye Bye Blackbird

Words by Mort Dixon
Music by Ray Henderson

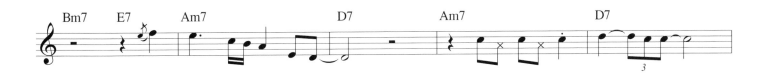

Doxy

By Sonny Rollins

C

D

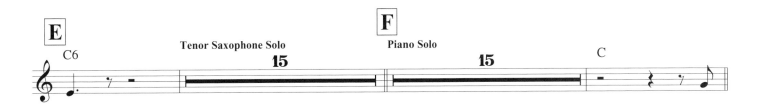

E.S.P.

By Wayne Shorter

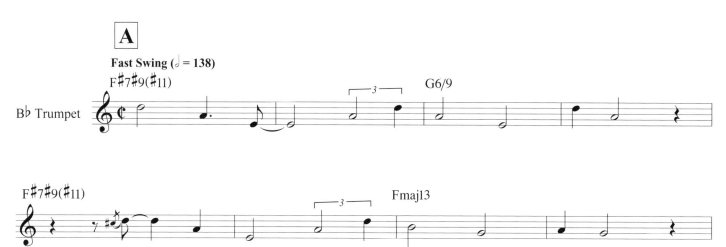

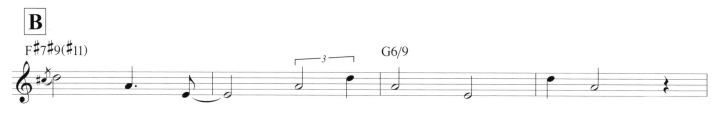

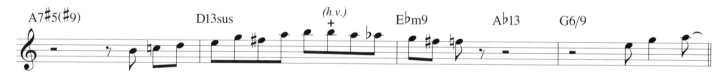

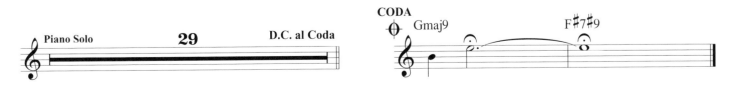

Half Nelson

By Miles Davis

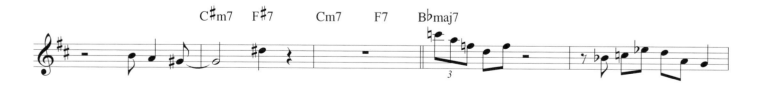

Move

By Denzil De Costa Best

So What

By Miles Davis

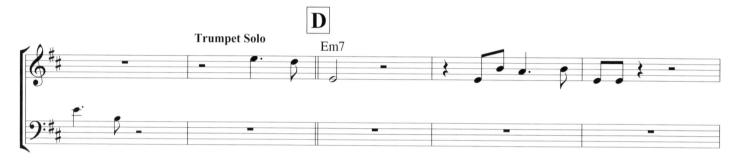

Summertime

from PORGY AND BESS ®

Music and Lyrics by George Gershwin, DuBose and Dorothy Heyward and Ira Gershwin

HAL•LEONARD® TRUMPET PLAY-ALONG

The Trumpet Play-Along Series will help you play your favorite songs quickly and easily. Just follow the printed music, listen to the sound-alike recordings and hear how the trumpet should sound, and then play along using the separate backing tracks.

1. POPULAR HITS

Copacabana (At the Copa) (Barry Manilow) • Does Anybody Really Know What Time It Is? (Chicago) • Hot Hot Hot (Buster Poindexter) • Livin' La Vida Loca (Ricky Martin) • Ring of Fire (Johnny Cash) • Sir Duke (Stevie Wonder) • Sussudio (Phil Collins) • Will It Go Round in Circles (Billy Preston).

00137383 Book/Online Audio $16.99

2. TRUMPET CLASSICS

Ciribiribin (Harry James) • Feels So Good (Chuck Mangione) • Java (Al Hirt) • Music to Watch Girls By (Bob Crewe Generation) • Spanish Flea (Herb Alpert) • Sugar Blues (Al Hirt) • A Taste of Honey (Herb Alpert) • The Toy Trumpet (Raymond Scott).

00137384 Book/Online Audio $16.99

3. CLASSIC ROCK

All You Need Is Love (The Beatles) • Deacon Blues (Steely Dan) • Feelin' Stronger Every Day (Chicago) • Higher Love (Steve Winwood) • September (Earth, Wind & Fire) • Spinning Wheel (Blood, Sweat & Tears) • 25 or 6 to 4 (Chicago) • Vehicle (Ides of March).

00137385 Book/Online Audio $16.99

4. GREAT THEMES

Cherry Pink and Apple Blossom White (Perez Prado) • Deborah's Theme (Ennio Morricone) • Dragnet (Walter Schumann) • The Godfather Waltz (Nino Rota) • Gonna Fly Now (Bill Conti) • Green Hornet Theme (Al Hirt) • The Odd Couple (Neal Hefti) • Sugar Lips (Al Hirt).

00137386 Book/Online Audio $16.99

6. MILES DAVIS

Airegin • Bye Bye Blackbird • Doxy • E.S.P. • Half Nelson • Move • So What • Summertime.

00137447 Book/Online Audio $16.99

7. JAZZ BALLADS

Body and Soul • Easy Living • Everything Happens to Me • I Remember Clifford • Over the Rainbow • Stella by Starlight • They Can't Take That Away from Me • Where or When.

00137475 Book/Online Audio $16.99

HAL•LEONARD® CORPORATION

7777 W. BLUEMOUND RD. P.O. BOX 13819 MILWAUKEE, WI 53213

www.halleonard.com

Prices, contents, and availability subject to change without notice.

0516